# Your Purpose...God's Plan

## Fasting Towards Your Destiny

Evangelist Chandra Burrow

All scriptures are from the New Living Translation of the Holy Bible unless otherwise noted

Copyright © 2015 Holloman Publishing

ISBN: 978-0-9897274-5-7

ISBN: 0989727459

**PROVERBS 3:6** (NLT)

SEEK HIS WILL IN ALL YOU DO,
AND HE WILL SHOW YOU WHICH PATH TO
TAKE.

I give God all the honor and glory for the ability to write this book. The inspiration and blessings that will come forth because of this vision is from God. I pray that wisdom from the knowledge given to me from God draws you closer to the Creator. Glory to God for all that will be gained from reading this book. I bind all confusions or ill will towards this God inspired work, which was created to honor God and to give hope to the world.

I also want to thank my husband and children for their support. Toney, Jemella, David Samuel, and Daya I love you and may God continue to guide you. I also ask that God continues to bless and guide my adult children, step-children, and grandchildren.

# Title

Introduction    5

Who is God?    9

What is Covenant?    14

What is Love?    17

Purpose and Plans    21

Being a Disciple    24

Praise and Worship    29

Fasting and Prayer    31

Fasting Scriptures    37

Corporate Fasting    41

24 hour Fast    43

72 hour Fast    46

7 day Fast    52

21 day Fast    65

# Introduction

Ask yourself, "Why am I fasting?"

We should ask ourselves this question before entering into a Fast Covenant with God. The promise we make with God is an individual possibly one-sided binding contract. Comprehending why you are fasting, the purpose of the fast, and the power behind the fast is important and should be embraced. Gaining understanding (knowledge) propels us into our destiny using God's will and not our own (Proverbs 4:5-8). A Collective fast does not mean the rules of the Fast Covenant change. This is why you need to understand the purpose of a church wide (congregational) or collective fast, by asking God. God will reveal to you what He wants from you as an individual as well as the body collectively.

Do not fast because you want something from God that is not purposed for you. There are times when people seek God for selfish reason; which must be avoided (Matthew 6 and Proverbs 18:1-2). Record your journey during the fast in a journal. Recording the life changing events in and/or around your life while fasting will help you remember God's will and revelation. During your fast, even a short one, get a journal or recording device before you start and record every moment. I'm going to 21 days but you can reuse scriptures or meditate on one or as many scriptures as God shows you to complete your fast. Each scripture reflects humility, repentance, who God is, a covenant, love, purpose & plans, disciple attributes, praise & worship, and finally fasting & prayer. I hope that you will pray and let God lead you through this journey towards your purpose. This guideline will assist you in understanding your purpose through God's word while walking towards your destiny. If you don't understand why you are fasting or cannot answer the question of why you're fasting, that is okay. Be honest with yourself and seek God. We serve a loving Father, so God will understand what you need. We must let God know what we need through prayer. Remember prayer is having a conversation with God, so wait for God's response before you move forward.

Ask God:  "God (Lord) why am I fasting?"

"Am I supposed to fast?"

"Is this your will?"

During the days of fasting you can create your own questions for each day since this is a guideline to aid, if needed. Before you enter into a fasting covenant ask yourself these questions:

What is the purpose of my Fast?

What am I trying to gain, loose, complete, or lose during this Fast?

If I am complaining (mumbling and grumbling) about this Fast, will it be successful with a negative mindset?

Did I pray and listen to God before or daily during this Fast?

What did I learn or what revelation was revealed during this fast?

Did I journal or record daily during this fast?

Books and verse numbers were used to allow the reader to choose their own version of the Bible, promoting and encouraging you to use the Bible for your own understanding and to research for yourself.

I used the NLT version; which is my preference along with NKJV, MSG, AMP, and NRSV.

# Who is God?

Who is God?

_____

_____

Who is God to you?

_____

_____

God is our Creator. God is our Father. God is our...
Elohim or God is Jehovah in many forms. Jehovah-
Nissi, Jehovah-Rapha, Jehovah- Mekoddishkem,
and Jehovah- Shalom are a few Old Testament
names that were used to describe who God was to
them. Knowing the names of God benefits us in our
prayer life as well as our daily walk to overcome the
trials and tribulation we face. Understanding who
God is gives us power in this world.

Jehovah Nissi -The Lord My Banner

Jehovah Rapha -The Lord That Heals

Jehovah Mekoddishkem -The Lord Who Sanctifies You

Jehovah Shalom -The Lord Is Peace

The first question we should ask ourselves is, "Who is God to me?". Everyone has a different understanding or belief of who God is in their life. Just because you are a babe in Christ or haven't built a strong relationship with God your thoughts, responses, or lack thereof could be different so don't be ashamed or feel as if something was wrong. More often people only comprehend who God is through their parents, other Christians, or what is taught in the Church. It is not uncommon to only understand God as such or to think we are saved because we go to church, so don't be ashamed or give up on your journey. If you haven't said the prayer of salvation or been baptized let your church leader know and take the necessary steps to be saved. In the Bible, God is also referred to as the Creator, I AM, or Father. Knowing who God is can be answered through your personal relationship and this can change because of the season you are in. Relationship consists of spending time in prayer, reading, studying, and researching the word of God. Who God is and what God does within the Kingdom is very important during personal, corporate, and/or collective fasting.

Who God is to you or within you can only be defined by you through relationship, God's word, trials, and tribulation. Like any new relationship the more time you spend with the person or in this case God the definition or who God is will be to you. The more personal time you spend with God through prayer and studying the word of God will reveal who God is to you. The time you spend getting to know God never ends since this process is necessary for continuous growth. I hear people say, "They are not there yet," when speaking of others that have fallen or don't understand. I have always wonder where is "there"? Everyone is at a different level with God, but we are never free from making mistakes or succumbing to that which tempts us. If you ever get to a place where you believe that you are "there", you could be headed for a fall (Proverbs 11:2 and16:5). This type of thinking puts us in a place of pride and the enemy is waiting to attack or use us to attack others (Proverbs 16:18). Regardless of how long you've been in relationship with God you're not immune to falling for the tricks of the enemy in your humanness. Building your faith and wisdom with the Creator never ends as long as you're alive. When Pastors, Preachers, or Church leaders fall they have lost focus. The enemy tempts them with their own fleshly desires; therefore, keep them covered in prayer. The temptation is easier when pride or haughtiness is present. Praying for our leaders should be done often during corporate fasting, because the enemy wants to destroy the Church through our leaders. Leaders are not perfect, but imperfect beings being used by God to oversee God's people; yet are to be above reproach(1 Timothy 3:2). Fasting is a time of revelation for you so discernment is optimized during this time. Stay focused on God and see how God reveals who He is to you.

In 2 Corinthians 12 Paul talks about the thorn in his flesh. This reminded him to stay humble Humility is nessecary for us to connect with God through prayer. If we are not humble, our prayers are not righteous.

# What is a Covenant (בְּרִית / διαθηκη)?

A covenant is considered an agreement between God and God's people. God has already given us the conditions of these covenants and will bless us through the covenant set forth for those that believe. It is up to you as an individual to keep the covenant conditions to receive the blessings of that covenant from God; although God will bless whom God choses to bless. Throughout the Bible, God has given man covenants that are either conditional or unconditional. Fasting is a covenant between you and God.

As mentioned in the introduction this guideline is to help guide you into your destiny. Look at this book as seeds being planted and/or water being poured to provide sustenance because God gives the increase and revelation in and over your life. I suggest that you read "The Eight Covenants Of The

Bible" by Dr. Arnold G. Fruchtenbaum to learn more about the different covenants and their importance.

## What is the purpose of your Fast Covenant?

Comprehending why you're entering into a Fast Covenant will give you an insight towards your destiny and the purpose for Fasting in that season. Knowing how long or how you should fast is between you and God, unless it's a corporate/collective fast. There will be times when you enter into a Fast Covenant because you need clarity or don't understand what you need and that is okay. As children of the Most High God, we look to our father for everything we need if you need anything, including understanding and clarity. Prayer should be your first step. Seek God through prayer at all times while fasting. This allows you to uphold the personal covenant you have enter into with God. You will also receive the answers you need and the revelations God has for you.

<u>When you enter into a covenant with God, the covenant should never be taken lightly</u>; whether it's personal, congregational, or collective with other believers. We are seeking God's will and direction for our lives and ministry; therefore, we should always go before the Creator with humility and a contrite heart (Psalm 51:17).

# What is Love?

What does your love say to others in the Kingdom or the world?

Do you walk in a Godly (unconditional or Agape) love?

Does your love, honor God?

Is your love conditional?

The two greatest commands are based on love; therefore, our lives should exemplify unconditional and agape love towards man, ourselves, and God (Matthew 22:36-40). This love should be towards God first and secondly, our neighbor (the world). The only time this causes an issue is when we don't love ourselves. Loving God is impossible if you don't love yourself. God is love and because God created us in His image and of Them within the Holy Trinity (Genesis 1:26-27), we should love the attributes God so loving created within us.

1 Corinthians 13 are the characteristics of love; thereforewithot the action of love we have nothing. This type of love starts with God, but ultimately ends with you. If you don't love you, how can you love the God that created you in His image or your neighbor that you are to love unconditional? God dwells within us through the Holy Spirit; so saying we love ourselves while contaminating our temple (body) with worldly or fleshly toxins we are lying to ourselves. What worldly or fleshly toxins are you allowing into your temple? I am not referring to the things man told you to stop doing, but the things that the Holy Spirit has warned you about. God loves you so much that He wants to cleanse you but you must be a willing vessel. Sometimes we get so caught up in what man is saying we negate the voice of God; consequently, allowing our flesh to decide what we are to do. When this is done, we are trying to become or fulfill the purpose of Jesus;

which is impossible. Man doesn't have the ability to fulfill the laws set and God knew this because of our sinful nature at birth this is why Jesus was sent (Genesis 8:21).

<u>When we think of love we see a romantic or relational love with friends and family, but God wants us to embrace unconditional and agape love with others.</u>

There are times when some Christians get so caught up in the cries of the crowd the spirit of hate and condemnation of others takes over; consequently, the person and not the sinful actions are hated and condemned. In our humanness this can be easy to do; therefore, we must have an accountability partner, so we can repent and stay on track. Some of these fights are not worth your response. God has already warned us about what will happen in this world, so spreading love instead of judgment will draw the sinner to Christ. If a person wants to continue to deny God, because God gave man the freedom of choice or they have given over to their reprobate minds; consequently, love through prayer may be needed (Romans 1: 18-32).

Do you love yourself? If not remind yourself of whom God said you are and what you mean to God.

Remind yourself of this daily by reading these scriptures aloud in the mirror:

- Psalm 139:13-15
- Ephesians 2:10
- Ephesians 5:29
- Romans 8:26
- John 15:9

*If Jesus came to serve, who are we not to follow the example of serving others in love as we spread the Good News?*

# Purpose and Plans

What is your purpose?

_____

What are your plans to fulfill that purpose or how
have you planned to reach that goal?

_____

_____

_____

Now that you've written you plan, read Proverbs
14:12 and 16:25. I'm not saying that you shouldn't
write your plans down as stated in Habakkuk 2:2
but seek God first. Before you write anything down,
while you're writing, after you write, and as the
process is being carried out; seek God at all times.
Read Habakkuk 1 through 3 to gain the wisdom

God has for you through the knowledge (reading and comprehending) of scripture. I was once told, "Knowledge understands that a tomato is a fruit, but wisdom knows not to put it in a fruit salad." When we gain knowledge (know how) but refuse to embrace wisdom (applying what you know) we choose to make poor choices. Our purpose is to honor God as Christians because we were created by the creator and chosen by God to give Him glory.

We were created to glorify God; therefore, if your purpose doesn't give God glory or hope to direct others to God, seek God for clarity. The way you are being used for the edification of the kingdom is revealed by God through the Holy Spirit, but man will tell you what or how you should do the will of God; therefore seek God for clarification. Man will say what's not of God or that God doesn't approve of what you are doing, because of where they are in their walk with God and. Do not let man hinder you from the path God has given you. Our paths are hindered by our flesh or the flesh of others; therefore, before moving forward seek God first for revelation and confirmation. God can and will send others to confirm or give you revelation, but allow God's plan to work as stated in Ephesians 1:11.

# Being a Disciple

Read John 13:35.

Jesus wanted us to understand that our love towards others within the Kingdom will show the world who we serve; therefore, being a disciple is important. We learn about discipleship in most brick and mortar churches we attend, but some churches do not focus on how love honors God as a disciple. Some Christians are so busy fighting about how to serve God or which denomination is right, they forget that love covers all (1 Peter 4:8-11). We can serve the same God and read the same Bible, but flesh can hinder God's will.  A disciple means more than just believing in God, we are to honor God through our service, works and actions (Luke 9:23).

I was reading a post on a social media group that I'm a part of. A member asked if we could use the big G when referring to God. I found this to be a little strange. The greater works was that people were talking about God. After her comment a few people became outraged over the correction. Some people do not comprehend why we believe or there arebelievers that are on the fence, so they can get offended by what is not known or not understood. The best part of the feed was when non-believers were intrigued by God's greatness. Sometimes Christians get so caught up in simple things we miss the bigger picture. Gaining understanding on when and how to correct as a disciple is very important. I must admit I too struggle with that at times.

Jesus did not make it easier to follow the law or to be a disciple when He walked with the Disciples, so they could embrace the New Covenant which was spreading the good news of grace and mercy (Matthew 5; 10:34-39). The new covenant of grace and mercy came after Jesus died and ascended into heaven therefore the New Covenant starts in Acts. The New Covenant doesn't give us a pass to sin (Romans 5: 12-6), therefore a disciple should:

- Believe the gospel
- Is not willing to compromise their convictions to satisfy themselves or others.
- Be a student of Christ.
- Be willing to sacrifice their fleshly goals for God's will
- Desires to put God first so that God's will is done.
- Absorbs the true gospel.
- Spreads the gospel to encourage and make disciples.
- Embrace and understand their spiritual gifts and/or appointment.

- A disciple imitates the example set forth by Jesus and the Agape love of God.

Remember to stay focused on God and not the things of this world, which is a major responsibility for disciples. Some people believe the more stuff they have…the more they're blessed, but never consider that the blessings they have are to glorify and honor God by being a blessing to others. I am not saying you have to live like a pauper, but you should ask God what to do with what you have blessed with. Knowing your spiritual gift/s is important. If you are a giver you may give more freely than others, but that does not make others less than you i8n the eyes of God. Your spiritual gifts are described in 1 Corinthians 12. Your duties according to your spiritual gifts are in Romans 12:3-13. Don't confuse spiritual gifts with the spiritual appointments given in Ephesians 4:11-16. Don't get caught up in someone else's blessing by thinking you are not blessed because you do not have what they have.  God gives as God sees fit.

Read 2 Timothy 2:15-26 and Romans 9:1-29. Record what God reveals to you.

_____

_____

_____

_____

_____

_____

_____

# Praise and Worship

Although, praise and worship are under the same heading they are two separate acts.

When we praise God, it comes from the thoughts of how awesome God has been to us. This is why we honor God with the joyful bliss we have for what God has done for us openly to others (Romans 15:11). While in the position of praise we tend to express joy in an outward action. This does not mean that if you're not loud or seen by others you're not praising God. Everyone's actions are different, yet there has to be some type of action to exhibit the act of praise unto God, even if it's softly or quietly vocal (Luke 19:40).

Worship is the spiritual connection we enter into with God. Our actions may or may not be seen by others (John 4:23). Worship is the feeling you have inwardly. When you think of the glory or goodness of God you embrace the respect, honor, and adoration you have for God. This comprehension is deep and personal because it is between you and God alone (Psalm 29:2).

I've always viewed praise as the burnt offering we give God and worship as the fragrant scent of that offering. Express your act of praise with a reverent spirit of worship daily during your fast. Praise and worship go hand in hand daily as we humble ourselves in reverence unto God while fasting.

# Fasting and Prayer

In my opinion, I don't believe you can fast without prayer and studying God's word because then it's just a diet. Again that's my opinion, which means it is not biblically sound; therefore, however God has instructed you to fast that is what you should do. We have been taught that Fasting means going without something, but the church has incorporated adding something. This is a great opportunity to build your relationship with God by reading the word more, praying more, or/and dwelling with God more. Before choosing a fast we must seek God on what or how long we should fast. In most churches, fasting is done yearly, which can cause some people to go with the motions and/or complain about fasting. When this happens, we have lost focus on the purpose of why we are fasting and need to get back on track. We need to help our brother's and/or sister's stay on track as well. This does not exclude the Pastor because we all need correction sometimes. If you do not receive the knowledge and wisdom it takes to correct your Shepherd or Church Leader and you think it is uncomfortable, you need to examine yourself. If your Shepherd or Church Leader rebukes you because of correction go to a Church Elder. If talking to the Elder(s) does not work seek God and pray for them (1Timothy 5:17-22 and Matthew 7:15-20). Correction and judging are different. We must remember those called to Shepherd are not perfect and can make mistakes because they are human beings, yet are told to have more self-control because of their responsibility to those they were called to serve (1Timothy 3:2).This does not include you religious beliefs but sound doctrine from the Bible.

Some believe that fasting is not mandatory according to the New Testaments, but it has become a tradition in the Church. This convent helps Christians seek spiritual focus, fulfills the needs of the Church body, and frees us from spiritual bondage just to name a few; therefore fasting is a personal choice between you and God.

Read Acts 13: 1-3 and 14:21-28.
Fasting and prayer is a powerful asset for us to use in the Kingdom.

Praying and fasting for the things our flesh wants give us glory and pleasure; therefore it is not a good reason to fast. We should focus on God's will for our lives, in this way God gets the honor and glory in every area of our life (1 John 5:13-17). If you are fasting for the desires of your heart you are fasting for the will of God to be done (Psalm 37:4). God keeps His word and will give you the desires of your heart, but you must first seek God (Matthew

6:25-34). When we seek the Kingdom of God our desires, wants, and needs will change causing us to desire the things of God and the Kingdom. When you seek to have an intimate relationship with the Creator your mindset and thoughts change; therefore, you become a new creation. You are not the person you were before you started your walk with Christ (2 Corinthians 5:11-15 & Isaiah 58:1-5). If you want to be certain that you are praying for God's will, ask God through pray or read God's word and it will be revealed to you. The biggest confirmation is when others see the change in you that is also a confirmation.

Read John 15:5-8

There are several types of prayer, yet they all allow us to have a conversation with God. After you pray wait for God to respond with an answer (revelation) before you walk away, if possible. When you want to learn how to pray ask God and study the Word. Look through Psalms and study the humility and faith David went before God with. David is a great example of having a contrite heart and faith in God. With the New Covenant we are to pray for our enemies, not against them as David did, so our enemies can see the God we serve and God's will being done. We do not want our hurt, pain, or anger for others to go forth through prayer unless we are asking God to help us(Matthew 5:43-48).

The New Covenant focuses on love not hate or an eye for an eye. We should always pray in love towards those that have wronged us, even when they cut us off in traffic.

What is your purpose for prayer?

_____

_____

_____

Do you need to find your purpose?

_____

- Do you need help with transportation?

---

- Do you need help with a co-worker or supervisor?

---

- Do you need help in your marriage/ family?

---

These are just a few things people pray about, although these prayers may not seem to edify the Kingdom they do, because of the impact these things have on our lives or our focus with God. They are necessary because we can't do anything without God. We get our strength, hope, and help from God. Prayers like this are needed to make us whole and distraction free, so we can be useful in the Kingdom (Philippians 4:6-7).

Read and meditate on John 14: 12-14, Luke 11:1-13, and1 Thessalonians 5: 12-18.

# FASTING SCRIPTURES

This is a guide for those new to fasting or a refreshing for others. This isn't the only way, but an effective way to reach a God given plan for your life. I want you to read the scriptures and research them for yourself to see what God is saying to you personally or how you should proceed (Psalm 18:30). This should be done anytime we read books based on God's truth or listen to sermons preached. God works on those that are called to preach first; while we are preparing sermons. This causes us to look inwardly first. After the revelation we are cleansed and properly prepared to give a word to God's people. That is why many are called, but few are chosen (Matthew 22: 1-14). This is why we should pray for one another and our Christian leaders daily; especially before and after the word of God is brought forth.

In our humanness we get caught up in what we are used to, what we have been taught is right, or what has become comfortable to us; which is natural but spiritually dangerous. Doing what we think is morally right may not be the same as following God's will or is spiritually right. The flesh of man gets caught-up in the education of others, the many profound words they use, or their titles. God's word lets us know, He can use the simplest things at times to confound the wise as stated in 1 Corinthians 1:27, so don't get caught up in who or what man is, but respect what God has called them to do.

When you open your eyes at the beginning of your day give thanks, honor, and praise to God. The alarm went off, so God opened your eyes and orchestrated your day. God does this by giving you another day filled with grace and mercy, so you have a fresh start to do God's will.

Each scripture for the fast reflects humility, repentance, and Who God is to you through Fasting and Prayer; therefore, pray and be guided by God as your purpose is revealed. This guideline was created to understand your purpose while walking towards your destiny following God's truth. If you don't comprehend why you're fasting or can't answer the question listed that is okay, but be honest with God. We serve a loving God; therefore, God will understand what you need and reveal it to you, so you must let God know by asking Him.

<u>You can create your own question as this is a guideline to assist.</u>

Before you enter into a Fast Covenant ask yourself these questions:

- What is the purpose of my Fast?
- Will I honor or glorify God during this fast?
- What am I trying to gain, loose, complete, or lose something during this Fast?

- Will I complain (mumbling and grumbling) about this Fast, is it going to be successful with a negative mindset?
- Will I pray daily during this Fast?
- What will I learn or revelation will I gain during this fast?
- Will I journal or record daily during this fast?
- What will I expect from this fast?
- Will I listen to God daily during this fast?
- Will I study during this fast?
- What knowledge will I gain during this fast?

**Before starting any type of fast that restricts your diet or requires you to do any type of physical exertion, consult your physician first; especially if you have any health issues.**

# Corporate Fasting

The attitude of a repenting and contrite heart sincerely seeking God allows God to come into worship with you.

The Bible is full of accounts where people came together to pray and/or fast for different reasons. These reasons included revelation, healing, spiritual growth or God's forgiveness. Today we also pray and fast for those reasons; therefore when our Pastor calls for a corporate fast we must be on one accord with the body. The Fast can differ according to the leader, yet during the fast we become one on a spiritual level. Corporate fasting should also include your children because we are raising our children to follow our example/belief (Jonah 3).

A Collective or Corporate Fast can consist of a smaller ministry within or outside of the larger congregation you belong to. These groups can also consist of you and a friend or friends, you and your husband and/or your family, you and your co-workers. Here are a few references that will prepare you for a corporate fast. (All of my reading comes from NLT. You can use any version you choose)

- 1 Samuel 7:5-6
- Ezra 8:21-23
- Nehemiah 9:1-3
- Joel 2:15-16
- Jonah 3:5-10

God wants us to have a heart that is sincerely seeking Him. The heart condition in which you go before with God is important; therefore, prepare your heart before you fast. This will keep you spiritually aware of the attacks that surround you and can cause you to stumble or distract you from the purpose of the fast. *Your focus is always imperative*.

- Isaiah 58
- Jeremiah 14
- 1 Corinthians 8

# 24 hour fast

Meditation Scriptures:

- Jeremiah 1:16; 22:9
- 2 Chronicles 7:14
- Ephesians 1: 5
- Luke 6:27-31
- Proverbs 19: 21
- Matthew 5:13-16
- Psalms 100:2; John 4:23
- Nehemiah 1:4
-

Repent for any act of disobedience/sin. We should ask for forgiveness for daily. What are the things you've put before God? Who did you seek for answers before seeking out God? Whom/what have you feared more than God (Losing your car, job, or your house, maybe it was your mate, Pastor/

Spiritual Leader, or Supervisor)? List them below or use your journal to record this journey.

_____

_____

_____

_____

_____

What are you seeking?

_____

_____

_____

_____

_____

_____

_____

# Revelations revealed?

# 72 hour fast

When you open your eyes at the beginning of your day give thanks to God because God has orchestrated your day by giving you another one. Repent, pray, praise, and worship

## Day 1

Meditation Scriptures:

- 2 Chronicles 7:14
- Acts 3:19
- Exodus 3:14
- Jeremiah 31:31-34
- 1 Corinthians 16:14
- John 6: 38
- 1 Corinthians 11:1
- Psalms 100:2; Exodus 20:2-6
- Esther 4:16

What baggage are you still carrying?

_____

_____

_____

_____

Why are you seeking God?

_____

_____

_____

_____

Revelations revealed?

_____

_____

_____

## Day 2

Meditation Scriptures:

- 2 Chronicles 7:14
- Acts 2:38
- Exodus 17:14-15
- Psalms 74:20
- Luke 6:35
- Colossians 1: 20-22
- Matthew 28:18-20
- 1 Corinthians 7:5
- Psalms 117:1-2

What baggage are you still carrying?

_____

_____

_____

_____

What are you seeking God for?

_____

_____

_____

_____

Revelations revealed?

_____

_____

_____

_____

## Day 3

Meditation Scriptures:

- 2 Chronicles 7:14
- Luke 13:3

- Jeremiah 23:6
- Psalms 105:8
- 1 John 4:7
- Proverbs 12: 5
- Romans 1:25
- Zephaniah 3:17
- Mark 9:29

What baggage have you given released?

_____

_____

_____

_____

Why are you seeking God?

_____

_____

_____

_____

# Revelations revealed?

# 7 DAY FAST

The number seven has a powerful significance in the Kingdom of God, it means completion. Completing things is a cause for celebration for you and those around you. Eight represents new beginnings; therefore, after you finish this fast you should look forward to the newness of your surroundings. While going into this fast focus on what you need to complete in your life or rid yourself of completely so that you can celebrate a new beginning.

There are things that we've left incomplete in our lives whether it good, bad, or indifferent and now is the time finish. Once we complete unfinished business we transcend towards another level in our life. Declare your victory by overcoming unfinished business. This unfinished business could be what hinders you from moving to the next level in Christ. Not taking care of unfinished business can hurt you. Incompleteness can affect getting that promotion you want, having financial blessings, being a blessing to others, or having peace within your life. Jesus had a purpose, and that was to serve, give a revelation, fulfill the law, and die for our sins. Once the journey was complete Jesus let the Father know that his work was finished. Once Jesus died there was a new covenant of grace and mercy that we have been given freely as long as we believe.

What work has God given you to complete? Do you understand your purpose? Are you on track to complete your assignment?

*This fast can be used to inspire competition or for whatever you choose. Remember the questions are just a guideline.*

## Day 1

Meditation Scriptures:

- 2 Chronicles 7:14
- 1 John 1:5-10
- Psalm 23:1
- Matthew 26:17-30
- Romans 12:8-12
- Proverbs 15: 21-22
- 2 Timothy 2:2-6
- Psalms 127:1-2
- Acts 13:1-4

What do you need to complete?

_____

_____

_____

What are you seeking God for?

_____

_____

_____

Revelations revealed?

_____

_____

_____

_____

## Day 2

Meditation Scriptures:

- 2 Chronicles 7:14
- 2 Peter 3:8-10
- Genesis 16:11-14
- Psalms 105:8-11
- John 8:12-15
- Ephesians 3: 14-21
- Acts 2:42-44
- Hebrews 13:14-15
- Mark 9:28-29

What are you committed to completing?

_____

_____

What are you seeking God for?

_____

_____

_____

_____

Revelations revealed?

_____

_____

_____

_____

## Day 3

Meditation Scriptures:

- 2 Chronicles 7:14
- Romans 2:1-11
- Exodus 6: 1-3
- Romans 9:7-9

- Mark 12:31
- Isaiah 14: 24
- Matthew 16:24-25 –
- Colossians 3:15-16
- Luke 2:37-38

Have you thought of a plan to complete your unfinished business?

_____

_____

_____

What are you seeking God for?

_____

_____

_____

Revelations revealed?

_____

_____

# Day 4

Meditation Scriptures:

- 2 Chronicles 7:14
- Genesis 4: 3-7
- Judges 6:24
- Jeremiah 33: 19-22
- Romans 12:9
- John 6: 35-40
- John 8:31-32
- Ephesians 5:15-20
- Matthew 6:16-18

Have you completed anything?

_____

_____

_____

_____

_____

Why are you seeking God?

_____

_____

_____

_____

Revelations revealed?

_____

_____

_____

_____

## Day 5

Meditation Scriptures:

- 2 Chronicles 7:14
- Isaiah 58:1-14
- Ezekiel 48:30-35
- Hebrews 6:18

- Romans 13:8-10
- Jeremiah 29: 11
- Ephesians 4:11-17
- Isaiah 25: 1
- Joel 1:14

What have you completed?

_____

_____

_____

_____

Why are you seeking God for?

_____

_____

_____

_____

Has God revealed any revelations to you?

_____

_____

_____

_____

_____

## Day 6

Meditation Scriptures:

- 2 Chronicles 7:14
- 1 John 1:9
- Exodus 31:13
- Matthew 26:28
- 1 Corinthians 13:4-8
- Romans 8: 28
- Luke 6:40
- Hebrews 13:15
- Joel 1:14

How did you feel during this journey of completion?

_____

_____

_____

_____

Has what you were seeking God for changed?

_____

_____

_____

_____

Did the revelations surprise you?

_____

_____

_____

# Day 7

Meditation Scriptures:

- 2 Chronicles 7:14
- Acts 17:30
- 1 Thessalonians 3:11
- Hebrews 9:11-15
- Ephesians 4:2
- Ecclesiastes 3: 1
- 1 Corinthians 11:1-3
- Psalms 30:11
- Isaiah 58:6

What did you complete?

_____

_____

_____

_____

_____

_____

How did you feel during this journey?

_____

_____

_____

_____

_____

_____

Did your revelation line up with your purpose,

destiny, or your completed task?

_____

_____

_____

_____

_____

# *21 DAY FAST*

It has been said, it takes 21 days to break a habit. What habits are you trying to break? *This fast can be used to break a habit or for whatever you choose. Remember the questions are a guideline to assist you.*

## Day 1

Meditation Scriptures:

- 2 Chronicles 7:14
- Isaiah 64
- Numbers 23:19
- Isaiah 55:11-12
- 1 John 4:7
- Exodus 9: 16
- Psalm 18:30
- Psalms 100:4
- Joel 2:12

Do you have any habits?

_____

_____

_____

_____

What are you seeking God for?

_____

_____

_____

_____

What revelations did God reveal to you?

_____

_____

_____

# Day 2

Meditation Scriptures:

- 2 Chronicles 7:14
- 1 John 1:9
- Daniel 7:22
- John 15: 5-8
- 1 John 4:18-19
- Psalm 17:3
- Matthew 28:18-20
- Psalms 95:1-6
- Ezra 8:21-23

Did you find any habits?

_____

_____

_____

_____

What are you seeking God for?

_____

_____

_____

_____

Which revelations have you embraced?

_____

_____

_____

_____

## Day 3

Meditation Scriptures:

- 2 Chronicles 7:14

- 1 John 1:9
- Isaiah 54:5
- 1 Peter 1: 6-7
- Deuteronomy 11:13-22
- Philippians 2:3- 5
- 2 Timothy 2:2
- Psalms 127:3
- Isaiah 58:6

Which habits are you struggling with?

_____

_____

_____

What are you seeking God for?

_____

_____

_____

Did God reveal any revelations to you?

_____

_____

_____

## Day 4

Meditation Scriptures:

- 2 Chronicles 7:14
- Acts 2:38
- Genesis 22:14
- Daniel 7:18
- 1 Peter 4:8
- John 6: 40
- Luke 14:27
- Psalms 96:1-9
- Philippians 4:6-7

Which habits did God reveal to you?

_____

_____

_____

_____

What are you seeking God For?

_____

_____

_____

Have you accepted the revelations God revealed to you?

_____

_____

# Day 5

Meditation Scriptures:

- 2 Chronicles 7:14
- Revelation 2:5
- Revelation 16:7
- Jeremiah 18: 1-10
- John 15:13
- Psalm 57: 2
- Luke 9:23
- Psalms 95:1-6
- 1 Thessalonians 5:17

Did you know these were habits?

_____

_____

_____

_____

What are you seeking God for?

_____

_____

_____

_____

Did you receive any revelations?

_____

_____

_____

_____

## Day 6

Meditation Scriptures:

- 2 Chronicles 7:14

- Proverbs 28:13
- Psalm 23:1
- Matthew 7:11
- Psalms 127:1-2
- Proverbs 20: 18
- Hebrews 12:5-11
- Revelation 15:4
- Acts 13:2

Which habits were negative?

_____

_____

_____

_____

What are you seeking God for?

_____

_____

Revelations revealed?

_____

_____

_____

_____

## Day 7

Meditation Scriptures:

- 2 Chronicles 7:14
- James 4:8-10
- Jeremiah 32:27
- Nehemiah 9:38
- Matthew 6:26
- 2 Corinthians 10:3-5
- John 13:34-35
- John 4:24
- Matthew 9:14-15

Which habits were positive?

_____

_____

_____

What are you seeking God for?

_____

_____

_____

What revelations are you uncomfortable
embracing?

_____

_____

_____

## Day 8

Meditation Scriptures:

- 2 Chronicles 7:14
- Isaiah 45:9
- Acts 4:24
- Exodus 6:1
- Colossians 3:14
- Ecclesiastes 3: 11
- Luke 14:33
- Psalm 150:6
- Acts 14:23

Which habits were useful in the Kingdom?

_____

_____

_____

_____

What are you seeking God for?

_____

_____

_____

_____

## What revelations were revealed to you?

_____

_____

_____

_____

## Day 9

Meditation Scriptures:

- 2 Chronicles 7:14
- Hebrews 9:14-15
- 1 Timothy 1:17

- 2 Peter 3:9
- Ephesians 5:25
- Proverbs 4: 25
- Luke 14:26
- Psalm 68:4-5
- 2 Samuel 12:15-17

Which negative habits have hurt you?

_____

_____

_____

What are you seeking God for?

_____

_____

_____

Were any revelations revealed to you?

_____

_____

_____

_____

## Day 10

Meditation Scriptures:

- 2 Chronicles 7:14
- 2 Corinthians 5: 18-21
- Psalm 68:4-5
- Romans 10: 4
- Proverbs 10:12
- Galatians 1: 3-4
- John 15:1-17
- Romans 14:11
- Psalm 35:13-14

Which habits would you like to stop doing?

_____

_____

_____

_____

What are you seeking God for?

_____

_____

_____

_____

Where revelations revealed to you?

_____

_____

_____

# Day 11

Meditation Scriptures:

- 2 Chronicles 7:14
- 2 Corinthians 7:9-11
- John 20:28
- Matthew 26:28
- Psalm 18:1
- Isaiah 42: 6
- Matthew 4:1-11
- Romans 11:36
- Daniel 10:3

Which habits has God been trying to remove from your life?

_____

_____

_____

_____

What are you seeking God for?

_____

_____

_____

_____

What revelations were revealed to you?

_____

_____

_____

_____

## Day 12

Meditation Scriptures:

- 2 Chronicles 7:14

- Ezekiel 18:21-23

- Luke 2:29

- Ecclesiastes 3: 17

- 1 Corinthians 13:13

- Ephesians 5: 15

- Acts 20:29-31

- Psalm 42:11

- Mark 1:35

Do you believe that God will help you eliminate negative habits?

_____

What are you seeking God for?

_____

_____

_____

_____

What revelations were revealed to you?

_____

_____

_____

_____

## Day 13

Meditation Scriptures:

- 2 Chronicles 7:14
- Luke 13:3
- 1 Samuel 1:3
- Genesis 9:16
- Ephesians 5:33
- Isaiah 46:10-11
- 1 Corinthians 2: 16
- Psalm 66:17

- 1 Kings 21:27-29

Are you working on the habits God has shown/told you to eliminate?

_____

_____

What are you seeking God for?

_____

_____

_____

_____

Which revelations were reveal to you?

_____

_____

_____

## Day 14

Meditation Scriptures:

- 2 Chronicles 7:14
- Acts 3:19
- Psalm 91:1-2
- Isaiah 24:5
- Proverbs 17:17
- Proverbs 16: 4
- John 6:45
- Daniel 4:37
- Jonah 3:5-10

How does it feel to work towards a goal that is God inspired?

_____

_____

_____

_____

What are you seeking God for?

_____

_____

_____

_____

Revelations revealed?

_____

_____

_____

_____

## Day 15

Meditation Scriptures:

- 2 Chronicles 7:14
- Acts 17:30

- John 4:9-14
- Hosea 6:7
- 1 John 3:16-18
- Isaiah 46: 10
- 2 Peter 1:1
- James 3:10
- Psalm 107:28-30

Will you continue to strive, so that habit will not overtake you?

_____

What are you seeking God for?

_____

_____

_____

_____

_____

Revelations revealed?

_____

_____

_____

_____

## Day 16

Meditation Scriptures:

- 2 Chronicles 7:14
- Acts 3:19
- Isaiah 45:18
- Genesis 21:27
- John 3:16
- Ephesians 1: 5
- Leviticus 20:7
- Revelation 5:13
- Acts 13:3

Who is your accountability partner that will help you during this cleanse?

_____

_____

_____

_____

What are you seeking God for?

_____

_____

_____

_____

Do you understand the revelations that were revealed to you?

_____

_____

# Day 17

Meditation Scriptures:

- 2 Chronicles 7:14
- 1 John 1:9
- Daniel 7:25
- Hebrews 6: 17
- 1 John 4:8
- 2 Corinthians 10:3-5
- Titus 3:14
- Psalm 95:6
- Matthew 21:22

How many habits have you eliminated so far?

_____

What are you seeking God for?

_____

_____

Have you embrace these revelations revealed to you?

_____

_____

_____

_____

## Day 18

Meditation Scriptures:

- 2 Chronicles 7:14
- Luke 24:47
- Revelation 6:10
- 2 Samuel 5:3
- Matthew 22:27-29
- 1 John 2: 17
- 1 Peter 1:15-16

- Psalm 119:7
- James 5:14-16

You are coming out of the bondage of your habit, so do you feel lighter?

_____

_____

_____

What are you seeking God for?

_____

_____

_____

Do you comprehend the revelations revealed to you?

_____

_____

# Day 19

Meditation Scriptures:

- 2 Chronicles 7:14
- 1 Kings 5:12
- Ephesians 2:18
- Isaiah 24:5
- Matthew 6:24
- Proverbs 15: 22
- Psalms 37:21
- Psalm 71:8
- Acts 9:40

Are you praising God for the release?

_____

_____

_____

_____

What are you seeking God for?

_____

_____

_____

Revelations revealed?

_____

_____

_____

## Day 20

Meditation Scriptures:

- 2 Chronicles 7:14
- Matthew 3:8
- Jeremiah 16:19
- Psalms 105:8
- Deuteronomy 10:12-13

- Ephesians 3: 10-11
- Matthew 11:29
- Daniel 2:23
- Mark 11:24

How many habits did you overcome?

_____

_____

_____

_____

What are you seeking God for?

_____

_____

_____

_____

What revelations were revealed to you?

_____

_____

_____

_____

## Day 21

Meditation Scriptures:

- 2 Chronicles 7:14

- Revelation 3:19

- 1 Thessalonians 5:23-24

- Isaiah 54:10

- Matthew 22:37-39

- Acts 11: 23

- Psalms 34:14

- Psalm 19:1-2

- James 5:14-16

Celebrate being a conqueror. Do you feel like a conqueror?

_____

_____

What did you conqurer?

_____

_____

_____

Celebrate the revelations revealed by God!!! List them below

_____

_____

# Notes

# Notes

# Notes

www.ingramcontent.com/pod-product-compliance
Lightning Source LLC
Chambersburg PA
CBHW032046040426
42449CB00007B/1003

This book is more than a collection of short stories from the barber shop; it is a grander story of a man shaped by God, who turned a profession into a passion for serving and loving people. Martin Luther King, Jr. once said, "If a man is called to be a street sweeper, he should sweep streets even as Michelangelo painted, or Beethoven composed music, or Shakespeare wrote poetry. He should sweep streets so well that all the hosts of heaven and earth will pause to say, 'Here lived a great street sweeper who did his job well.'"

He pursues excellence in every haircut, but more importantly, he cares deeply for every person who's ever sat in his chair. He may never get the title of "best barber ever" from the world, but in my opinion, he might be the greatest barber of all time.

—**Logan Mabe**, Pastor, Ocean View Church,
Chula Vista

Have you ever met someone whose countenance makes you do a double-take and causes you think, *That's a phenomenal human being*? Lakeith Jones is such a man.

He is the kind of man you unknowingly let your guard down around. Rub shoulders with him for one moment, and if you're not careful, you'll leave with a smile on your face. If he lived in my city, I'd demand he be my barber. He wrote this book about the numerous encounters he has had refreshing the souls of well-groomed customers, and that's one book I would happily invest in.

—**Caleb Sonneman**, Navy Veteran